W9-BWJ-956

Nature's Fury

AVALANCHES

John Hamilton

ABDO
& Daughters

VISIT US AT

WWW.ABDOPUB.COM

Published by ABDO Publishing Company, 4940 Viking Drive, Suite 622, Edina, Minnesota 55435.
Copyright ©2006 by Abdo Consulting Group, Inc. International copyrights reserved in all countries.
No part of this book may be reproduced in any form without written permission from the publisher.
ABDO & Daughters™ is a trademark and logo of ABDO Publishing Company.

Printed in the United States.

Editor: Paul Joseph
Graphic Design: John Hamilton
Cover Design: Neil Klinepier
Cover Photo: Corbis
Interior Photos and Illustrations:

    Corbis, p. 1, 3, 5, 6, 7, 8, 9, 10, 11, 12, 13, 14, 15, 17, 19, 20, 21, 23, 25, 26, 27, 28, 29
    AP/Wide World Photos, p. 4, 16, 24, 32

Library of Congress Cataloging-in-Publication Data

Hamilton, John, 1959–
    Avalanches / John Hamilton.
       p. cm. — (Nature's fury)
    Includes index.
    ISBN 1-59679-328-7
    1. Avalanches—Juvenile literature. I. Title.

    QC929.A8H36 2006
    551.3'07—dc22

                            2005049025

CONTENTS

AVALANCHE!

IN FEBRUARY 2005, IN THE MOUNTAIN VILLAGE OF VALTENGU, Kashmir, 40-year-old schoolteacher Bashir Malik stepped out of his house one snowy evening to run an errand. He'd only gone a short distance when he suddenly heard a deafening rumble in the hills above the village.

The ground under Malik's feet began to tremble. He turned back toward his home and gasped. An avalanche descended on the town like a wall of white death, burying everything in its path. Malik could only watch helplessly as his home and the homes of his neighbors were swept away by the river of snow. Malik lost all 13 members of his family that day. "How I survived is a miracle," he later told a reporter. "But what good is life for me now?"

Many of the houses in the village were buried under heaps of heavy snow. Some victims were crushed in their collapsed homes. Others were carried off by the avalanche. They died horrible deaths, either by being hit by debris or suffocating under the packed snow. One witness described an ocean of snow sweeping everything away. In a matter of seconds, the avalanche killed 122 people, nearly one fourth of the entire village.

Valtengu lies in the Indian-controlled part of Kashmir. Unusually heavy snowfalls across the entire Himalayan region that winter triggered many avalanches. It was Kashmir's snowiest winter in 15 years. The area's remote location, coupled with the thick snow, made rescue efforts very

Victims of the February 2005 Kashmir avalanches gather near their destroyed houses.

An avalanche roars down a mountainside in the Karakoram Range, which includes part of Kashmir, a territory disputed by India and Pakistan.

difficult. More than 300 people were killed in the region, and many hundreds more were reported missing.

Deadly snow avalanches are a force of nature that can occur on any slope under the right conditions. These torrents of "white death" can descend mountainsides at frightening speeds. They've been killing for centuries, ever since people started settling in the mountainous regions of the world. On average, each year avalanches kill more than 150 people worldwide. Many thousands more are injured.

The alpine countries of France, Austria, Switzerland, and Italy have the most avalanches, and avalanche-related deaths, worldwide. One tragic trend in poorer countries is the building of villages higher and higher on mountain slopes, as people try to find more land for farming or firewood. Avalanches that would have slid harmlessly into remote wilderness areas are increasingly damaging human settlements.

The United States ranks fifth in avalanche deaths worldwide. Within the U.S., the most dangerous avalanche states are Colorado, Alaska, and Utah. In recent years, as winter recreation has become more and more popular, avalanche deaths have increased. Mountains attract tourists. People like to ski, climb, and snowmobile in mountainous areas. This puts them directly in the path of avalanches.

Avalanche experts strongly advise people who enjoy exploring America's wilderness backcountry to understand the possible danger they put themselves in. By recognizing the warning signs, people can safely enjoy the great outdoors and avoid becoming avalanche victims.

A home and crumpled car lie buried in snow after an avalanche in Montroc, France, in February 1999. Ten people were killed.

An avalanche of snow falls toward three climbers on Mount Everest, in the Himalaya Mountains.

WHITE DEATH

AVALANCHES CAN HAPPEN ON ANY SLOPE IF THE CONDITIONS are right. But in the United States, there are certain times and places that are more dangerous than others. Most people are killed by avalanches in wintertime, from December through March. The majority of deaths happen in January, February, and March. These are the months when the most snow falls in mountain areas.

Many deaths also occur in May and June, when spring melting causes avalanches. People get caught off guard because they wrongly think the nice weather protects them. Some avalanches even occur during early summer. Hikers are sometimes surprised by the amount of snow still remaining from winter.

Between 1950 and 1997, 514 people were killed by avalanches in the U.S. These deaths happened mainly in Western states. Colorado accounted for about a third of the fatal avalanches. By comparison, the northeastern U.S. has relatively few avalanches.

An avalanche warning sign in Glacier National Park, Montana.

The study of how and why avalanches occur is a complex subject. In a nutshell, all you need for an avalanche is a mass of snow plus a hill, or slope, for it to slide down. Think of a car windshield on a snowy day. Usually the snow sticks to the surface of the glass instead of sliding off. But when conditions such as wind or temperatures change, snow begins to slide down the glass in little slabs, like a miniature avalanche.

In the mountains, of course, avalanches happen for much more complex reasons, and on a much bigger

An avalanche response team practices a rescue drill.

scale. Some scientists estimate that a large North American avalanche releases up to 300,000 cubic yards of snow, enough to fill 20 football fields 10 feet (3 m) deep. Luckily, most people get caught in much smaller avalanches. But these can be just as deadly.

There are three main parts to an avalanche. Unstable snow fractures away from the surrounding snowpack in an area called the *starting zone*. These areas are usually found higher up the slopes, oftentimes beneath overhanging cornices of snow that form over rocky ridgelines. However, starting zone fractures can occur anywhere on a slope.

An *avalanche track* is the path an avalanche takes as it speeds down a slope. When people are crossing backcountry areas, it is important to be on the lookout for areas that look like avalanche "chutes," which are big vertical areas on the slope that are missing trees. These clearings are a good sign that avalanches have occurred here in the past, and will eventually happen again.

Runout zones are usually at the bottom of slopes, where avalanches finally come to rest. Snow and debris piles up in this fan-shaped area. Most victims of avalanches eventually are deposited in runout zones.

An avalanche crashes through the Savoia Pass on the northwest side of K2 in the Karakoram Range, Pakistan.

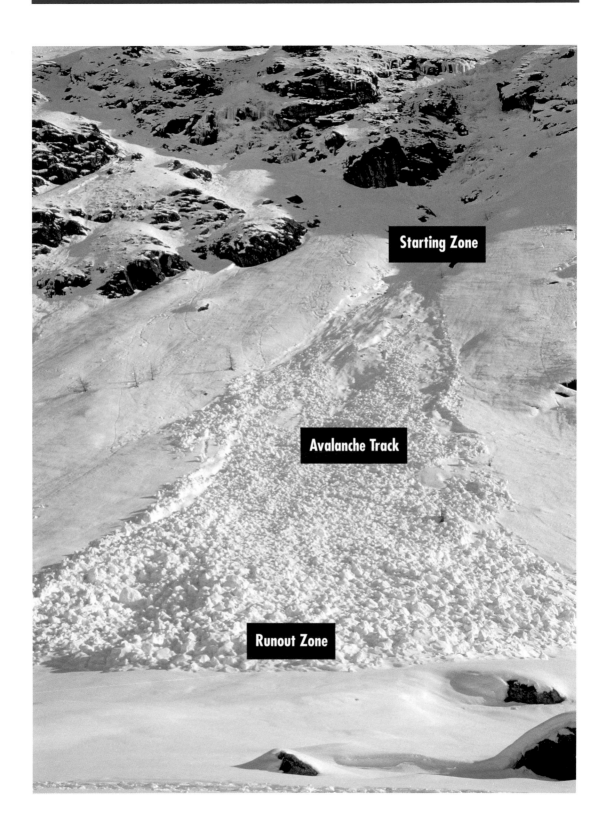

Starting Zone

Avalanche Track

Runout Zone

KINDS OF AVALANCHES

THERE ARE SEVERAL KINDS OF AVALANCHES. THE MOST DEADLY is called a *slab avalanche*. This happens when layers of snow under a snowpack fail and huge chunks slide downhill all at once. Since 1950, slab avalanches have killed more than 235 people in the United States.

Slab avalanches are big chunks of snow that break away as a single unit. The slab then breaks apart as it tumbles downhill. Scientists describe it like a pane of glass sliding off a tilted table. Slab avalanches are hard to see and avoid. Many people, especially skiers or snowmobilers, travel well into a slab before it fractures and begins falling, triggered by the weight of the unsuspecting victims themselves.

Another type of avalanche is the *loose snow avalanche*, which is also called a *sluff*. These usually occur on the surface

A mountain rescue team member stands near a windblown cornice.

of snowpacks, often after a new snowfall, or on wet spring snow. They start at a certain point on a slope and then spread out. Sluffs are seldom deep enough to bury people, although they can be strong enough to push skiers over cliffs.

Icefall avalanches are chunks of ice that fall off glaciers when they encounter a steep drop, like a cliff. As the glacier slowly moves downhill, these ice chunks "calf" off and plummet to the ground below. The best way to avoid being injured by an icefall avalanche is to simply avoid traveling beneath ice cliffs and glaciers.

Wind often blows across mountaintops and ridges, depositing snow on the opposite (leeward) side. This snow often forms cornices, which look like frozen waves stretching along the top of a ridge. A *cornice fall avalanche* occurs when this snow, which is dense and hard, yet surprisingly fragile, snaps off. When backcountry hiking, stay well away from the peaks of ridges. It is difficult to tell where the ground ends and the overhanging cornice begins. Once a cornice avalanche starts, there is additional danger of triggering a secondary slab avalanche farther down the hill.

An icefall avalanche in Torres del Plaine National Park, Chile.

WHAT CAUSES AVALANCHES?

MANY THINGS CAN CAUSE AVALANCHES. THE MOST OBVIOUS IS the force of gravity, but it's a bit more complicated than that. When snow falls on a slope, it sticks to the ground and clings there, forming a snowpack. If conditions change slowly, the snowpack stretches and stays put. But if a sudden force is applied to the snowpack, it snaps and causes an avalanche.

A snowpack is not a single blanket of white powder. By looking at a cross-section, we can see that it is made of many layers. Each layer represents a different weather event. Some snow layers are weaker than others. They contain different kinds of ice crystals. Some snow is shaped like the classic six-sided flake you usually think of. But other snow crystals look more like needles, or columns. Some resemble pellets, or grains of sand.

Wrecked cars litter a hillside after a fatal avalanche in Austria in February, 1999.

The most dangerous kind of snowpack has a strong layer of cohesive, "sticky," snow resting on top of a weak, unstable layer. That's when the danger of a slab avalanche is greatest. The top layer cracks off like a pane of glass and slips downhill on a layer of weak snow underneath.

Once an avalanche begins, it can plummet downhill incredibly fast, reaching speeds between 60 to 80 miles per hour (97 to 129 km/hr).

An avalanche at Ruth Glacier, Alaska.

Avalanche fatalities are often caused by the victims themselves, such as skiers or snowmobilers.

Unlike most natural disasters, almost all avalanche fatalities are caused by the victims. This usually happens when outdoor enthusiasts, such as skiers or snowmobilers, venture onto slabs of unstable snow.

This sudden additional weight puts enough stress on a snowpack to fracture a slab and send it, along with the helpless victim, tumbling downhill, oftentimes to a sudden death.

There are many things that can make a snowpack unstable. By observing your surroundings and the conditions of the snowpack, you can prevent disaster. Even the weight of a single skier can be enough to cause an unstable snowpack to turn into a deadly avalanche.

• WEATHER

Weather is a very important factor. The first 24 hours after a major snowfall are especially dangerous. Extra weight from a new layer of snow can be enough to cause an unstable slab to snap. In the mountains, snowfalls of one foot (.3 m) or more are common, and can be very hazardous. A snowfall amount between 6 and 12 inches (15 to 30 cm) can sometimes cause an avalanche, while anything less than 6 inches (15 cm) is usually not a threat.

A helicopter flies over an avalanche in Austria.

• TEMPERATURE

Snow is a good insulator. Small temperature changes, such as the shadow of a mountain passing over a snowpack, don't have much of an effect on the chances of an avalanche. Big changes in temperature, however, such as a warm front or spring warm-up, can weaken layers of snow, increasing the chances of an avalanche.

• WIND

Wind often blows up one side of a mountain or slope. This is called the windward side of a mountain. The wind scours surface snow, blowing it onto the other side of the mountain, which is the leeward side. Wind blown from one side of a slope to the other causes uneven snowpacks that are very prone to avalanches. These snowpacks are said to be *wind loaded*. Cornices, or icy overhangs, may build up on the mountain ridges, which is a sure sign of a wind-loaded mountainside. When traveling through the backcountry, it is almost always safest to travel on the windward side of the slope.

• SLOPE ANGLE

The angle of a slope, how steep it is, can affect the chances of an avalanche.

Most avalanches happen when a slope is at an angle between 30 and 45 degrees. Avalanches can happen on hills measuring more than 45 degrees, but it's harder for deep snow to accumulate on steeper slopes. But always remember that an avalanche can happen on even a gentle slope if the conditions are right. For example, wet snow is lubricated with water, and might cause an avalanche on a slope of only 10 degrees, which is nearly level terrain. An avalanche on such a gentle slope would be rare, but don't be fooled into thinking you're safe just because you're not on a steep slope!

• TERRAIN

The shape of the land can have a big impact on the likelihood of an avalanche. For example, big gullies or "bowl"-shaped areas accumulate snow quickly, increasing the chance of an avalanche. Vegetation can also play a role. Heavily forested areas are safer than wide-open spaces. Trees and other plants help stabilize the snow. However, sometimes avalanches start high up on the mountain, above the treeline, and then crash down into forests. When this happens often, a path, or "chute," is eventually cut through the forest. Beware when crossing these areas.

An avalanche snow chute in Banff
National Park, Alberta, Canada.

CONTROLLING AVALANCHES

THE DANGERS CAUSED BY AVALANCHES CAN BE LESSENED OR even eliminated with the right tools and techniques. Large walls, fences, or nets can be constructed to protect buildings, roads, or recreation areas from avalanches. Flat terraces are sometimes built into mountainsides, which break up the snowpack and help prevent dangerous slab formation.

Some mountain states, such as Colorado, Montana, and Utah, have special teams of people who search for areas where snowpacks are unstable. Instead of waiting for a disaster to catch unwary victims, these professionals cause avalanches under controlled conditions. Areas around highways or ski resorts are often prime candidates for man-made avalanches.

Park rangers shoot down potential avalanches with a recoilless rifle in Mount Baker National Forest, Washington.

Smaller avalanches are sometimes caused by skiing on the unstable snowpack. A safer and more common method is to use explosives. About one kilogram (2.2 pounds) of TNT is commonly used to set off an avalanche. The explosive is sometimes placed by hand where the experts want the slide to start. This can be extremely dangerous work. Helicopters are also used to drop bombs, but they can't fly in bad weather.

A safer method is to fire artillery shells, like those used by the army. A single weapon, such as a 105mm howitzer, can hit several targets rapidly from a safe distance. The Utah Department of Transportation fired about 550 explosive shells at mountainsides in 2004, safely causing controlled avalanches that might otherwise have slid down on their own and killed people. In an interview with the Weather Notebook radio show, Andy Gleason, who works for the Colorado Department of Transportation, said of the howitzer after witnessing it in action, "It's a good shot. The avalanche cracks three to four feet (.9 to 1.2 m) deep. As it slides, it takes out all the layers down to the ground. But the debris stops before it hits the road. Just what the avalanche control crew wants."

Avalanche barriers stand in an alpine field in Switzerland.

A TRUE-LIFE AVALANCHE STORY

WHAT IS IT LIKE TO BE CAUGHT IN AN AVALANCHE? BRUCE Tremper, a 24-year-old ski racer, found out the hard way in 1978. In November, shortly after graduating from college, he was helping build chairlifts at Bridger Bowl Ski Area in Montana. He was a very experienced skier. He had been skiing since he was a child, and thought he knew all about the dangers of avalanches.

One day, he went skiing alone, which isn't a good idea in avalanche country. More than a foot (30 cm) of snow had fallen the night before. The wind that day was blowing hard, loading up the slope with even more layers of unstable snow. To save time, Tremper decided to ski across a couloir, a mountain gully that can sometimes hide unstable snow. He thought that since he was such a good skier, he could speed across the snow before an avalanche occurred.

As Tremper later wrote, "Since I had never been caught in an avalanche before, I had no idea how quickly the slab can pick up speed after it shatters like a pane of glass. I heard a deep, muffled thunk as it fractured. Then it was like someone pulled the rug out from under me and I instantly flopped onto the snow, losing all the speed I had built up.

"So, like a startled cow, I sat there on my butt and watched soft slab instantly

A skier tries to outrun an avalanche on a Utah mountainside.

A skier is buried in powder as he makes his way down the mountain at Bridger Bowl Ski Area near Livingston, Montana.

shatter into little blocks and the blanket of snow rocketed down the slope as if sucked downward by the extra heavy gravity."

Tremper tried to ski out of the avalanche, but he found out it was like trying to ski on tumbling cardboard boxes. After only a couple of seconds, he was already traveling at about 20 miles per hour (32 km/hr). He tried to grab a small tree as he sped past, but couldn't grasp one. Finally he slammed into a tree and held on for dear life, but then the tree snapped and he started downhill again. By this time the avalanche had reached speeds up to 60 miles per hour (97 km/hr). Tremper said it was "like being stuck in a giant washing machine filled with snow. My hat and mittens were quickly ripped off along with both my skis. Snow went everywhere, down my neck, up my sleeves, down my underwear, even under my eyelids, something I would have never imagined." Even more seriously, snow began packing into his nose and mouth, creating a plug that was suffocating him.

Tremper started moving his arms and legs in a swimming motion, desperately trying to stay on the surface of the avalanche. Every time he stopped swimming, his body began sinking into the depths of the snow.

Finally, after what seemed like an eternity, the avalanche began to slow, and then finally settled at the bottom of the slope. Tremper found himself buried up to his waist, but miraculously, his head and arms were above the snow. He unplugged his mouth and could breath again. He considered himself very lucky, even though he was wet and cold.

Tremper had avoided being killed by striking an object, like a tree, on his tumble down the hill. Soon, however, he encountered another hazard of avalanches. As soon as the snow stopped moving, it hardened like quick-setting cement. Think of shoveling the pile at the end of your driveway after the snowplow has come by, and you can get an idea of how thick and heavy the snow is after an avalanche. It is almost impossible for people completely buried in an avalanche to dig themselves out. Their only hope is that someone will come to rescue them in time.

Luckily for Tremper, only his legs were buried by the avalanche. Still, it took many minutes to chip away the rock-hard snow and free himself. After this near-death experience, he decided to study avalanches, eventually landing a job on a ski patrol doing avalanche control.

Today Bruce Tremper is the director of the Forest Service Utah Avalanche Center in Salt Lake City, Utah. As he would later write, "I don't think it's possible to watch all the snow on a mountainside shatter like a pane of glass and roar to the bottom at 60 mph, ripping out trees, without it changing your life, especially if you triggered the avalanche, and more especially if you rode it down and survived."

Rescuers free a man buried by an avalanche in Austria.

AVALANCHE SAFETY

SNOW AVALANCHES ARE NATURAL PROCESSES. SOME SCIENTISTS estimate that they happen about one million times each year worldwide. They are not a problem until people get in the way. Avalanches don't usually fall from the sky onto unsuspecting victims. In 95 percent of cases where people are harmed by avalanches, it is because the people themselves triggered the snow slide.

The best way to survive an avalanche is to avoid one in the first place. There are three red flags you should always be aware of when skiing or snowmobiling in mountainous backcountry. These three warning signs are snowpack, terrain, and weather.

Mother Nature can give clues to unstable snowpacks. The most commonly overlooked clue is whether an area has previously had an avalanche. If there has obviously been a recent avalanche, stay well away from the area. Your own weight might be just enough to release more snow that didn't come down the first time. Also, if you are on a steep slope and hear hollow sounds or deep noises, there's a good chance the snow under you is beginning to collapse.

Shooting cracks and fractures are a sure sign that a slab is about to break off and tumble downhill. Another sign of danger

Rescue workers use long poles to search for buried victims of an avalanche in Switzerland.

An avalanche cascades down
a rocky mountainside.

is excess snow in the trees, especially from a recent snowstorm in the last 24 hours. Since snow hasn't had a chance to settle out of the trees, it's likely that it hasn't settled on the ground yet, either.

Terrain, the second red flag, is another warning sign that is relatively easy to spot. Beware of bowls and gullies. Steep slopes above the tree line can be especially dangerous. Areas that have experienced avalanches in the past often look like steep, treeless "chutes" that cut through forests. Beware when crossing areas like this.

Any rapid change in the weather makes an avalanche more likely. The most dangerous weather for causing avalanches is high winds, which can dump unstable snow onto areas 10 times faster than a normal snowstorm. Be especially wary of the windward side of slopes and ridges. High winds pick up snow from the windward side and deposit it on the other side. This creates unstable cornices and heavy layers of unstable snowpack. Heavy snowstorms, or rapid melting, can also bring down avalanches. Much depends on the condition of the snowpack to begin with. Most ski areas and outdoor park areas post alerts when snowpacks are unstable,

A man in Colorado examines layers of snow to determine the potential for an avalanche.

so pay attention to the warnings before venturing out into backcountry areas.

In the United States, most people who get caught in avalanches are outdoor recreationists, such as skiers, snowmobilers, snowboarders, or hikers. In most cases, it is the victim who triggers the avalanche. Once a victim is buried in the snow, there isn't much time to dig them out before they suffocate. Avalanche statistics show that most victims, about 93 percent, can survive if they are dug out within the first 15 minutes. After that, the survival rate drops quickly. After 45 minutes, only about 20 to 30 percent survive. After two hours, almost all victims die.

There are some tools that outdoor recreationists should always carry with them into avalanche country. These tools will add weight to your pack, but they can save lives. A lightweight portable shovel made of plastic or aluminum will decrease the time it takes to dig victims out of an avalanche. Once snow settles from an avalanche, it sets up like concrete. It is very difficult to dig out by hand.

Collapsible probes or ski-pole probes can be used to poke down into the snow to find avalanche victims. A more effective tool is an avalanche beacon. These are common rescue devices that help people on the surface rapidly locate someone buried in the snow. The victim's beacon transmits a radio signal. The signal is picked up by units on the surface switched to "receive." Rescuers move around on the surface in smaller and smaller circles until the signal is strongest, and then start digging. It's important to practice the proper technique and know how to use the equipment before setting out on any backcountry trip.

A newer hi-tech survival tool is a German-invented airbag system carried in a backpack. When inflated, two airbags pop out on either side of the victim's head and shoulders. The bags help keep victims from sinking in the moving snow. Today, the bags are most widely used in Europe. Of 70 cases where avalanche victims used their airbags, only three died. Avalanche experts in this country hope that the airbags catch on, despite their added cost.

Avalanches are a powerful and frightening reminder of nature's fury, but given the proper knowledge and equipment, most people in wilderness areas can safely enjoy the beauty of the backcountry.

A ski patrol member and his rescue dog practice digging victims out of the snow.

GLOSSARY

ALPINE

Something related to high mountains, like *alpine skiing*, or *alpine climbing*. The term refers to the European chain of mountains called the Alps, which stretch across many countries including Switzerland, France, Austria, and Italy, the four countries with the most avalanche-related deaths in the world.

AVALANCHE TRACK

The path an avalanche takes as it rumbles downhill. Avalanches often take the same path year after year. These areas often look like vertical, treeless gullies on steep slopes, and should be avoided when crossing wilderness areas. If an avalanche occurred in an area in the past, there's a good chance it will happen there again.

CORNICE

An overhanging layer of snow that forms on the top of rocky ridgelines. Wind usually blows in one direction across the top of the ridge, depositing snow on the opposite (leeward) side. As snow accumulates, the cornice looks like a frozen wave hanging over the top of the ridge. It is hard to tell where the ground ends and the overhanging cornice begins. A cornice fall avalanche occurs when this fragile snow snaps off and tumbles downhill.

COULOIR

Couloirs are shaped like large gullies and are found on the slopes of mountains. They can sometimes hide unstable snowpacks.

ICEFALL AVALANCHE
Icefall avalanches are hunks of ice and snow that fall off glaciers when they move over a steep drop, like a cliff.

RUNOUT ZONE
The area at the bottom of a slope where an avalanche eventually comes to rest. Snow and debris pile up in these fan-shaped areas.

SLAB AVALANCHE
The most dangerous kind of avalanche, slab avalanches happen when layers of snow under a snowpack fail and huge chunks slide downhill all at once.

SLUFF
Another name for a loose snow avalanche, which occurs on the surface of a snowpack, often after a new snowfall or wet spring snow. Sluffs aren't usually deep enough to bury people, but they can be strong enough to push skiers over cliffs.

STARTING ZONE
The area on a slope where an avalanche begins. Unstable snow fractures away from the surrounding snowpack and begins sliding downhill. Starting zones are usually high up, but can occur anywhere on a slope.

WEB SITES

WWW.ABDOPUB.COM

Would you like to learn more about avalanches? Please visit www.abdopub.com to find up-to-date Web site links about avalanches and other natural disasters. These links are routinely monitored and updated to provide the most current information available.

INDEX

An avalanche crashes through a forest in Switzerland.